# More Weight Than World

HR Sanger

1875

He watches her unwind
from the long journey.
Stepping from the train
in a honey-colored cloth,
the flowing material
so much softer
than her surroundings,
lingering
rustling
lingering
spinning slowly after
an immeasurable pace.
She and 1875the dress
move in a rose-like pattern,
the curling weave breathing on its own,
always after her,
eventually disappearing
around a corner.
With so many spinning bodies,
so many eyes beyond telescopic view,
he wonders,
what is this work,
among hidden
gradual galaxies?

As Body to Ghost

In his mind,
the small fire
        in the corner
of the room
  had escaped
        it's place
        and burned down
the surrounding walls
        many times.
Each time,
a spark ignited
            a new spot
                in the wallpaper.
 The first feeling
of comfort
   moved through him
            like smoke
    as he watched
  the figment flame
   gain intensity.
A transmutation:
     emotion to flame
         as body to ghost.
A true burning,
 even if imaginary
 and wanting only
 the first fifteen minutes
 of his consciousness.

Capital

The mechanical genius
that drives passengers through
the emaciated woodland,
is the same restless presence
that stalks the bookshelves in secrecy,
looking for answers to the intoxicating
queries spoken in sleep
by meandering middlemen,
those seeking an antidote to bribery,
a philosophy of equivalence,
a breed of pony which will take flight
and marry the horizon to casual currency.
The pathways are driven smooth.
The connecting points whisper
to one another, lengthwise.
There is much newness to blight the old,
bargaining again with small venture.
In the green corridors where the curious stand,
cities are stunted, bothered, or broken.
Cities are the half-thought of forsaken dreamers,
formulaic eccentricities drafted
for disquieting inhabitation.

Selfish Aquarium

Whether the participant can
perceive that order, embracing
communication in a multi-sensory
way is fully encouraged.
Using all tools
and seeking a meaningful
interpretation of the Actual
is a complete interaction.
Seeking to understand Actuality
means a divorce, or at least separation,
from man-made worlds.
To establish a center of gravity
in oneself and one's position
as a participant in experience,
one must seek Self
in relation to a limited system
of sensory perception.
Whatever the outcome,
our echoes must not come alive on the other side.

Too Early To Be Late


It's late.
It's too early to be late,
yet it's late.
It's too late to be early.
There's too much drift to hold still.
The clouded blue overhead,
too swollen for non-emergence.
Everything is born.
Everything lies down.
Everything, at some point, wonders why.

Only Your Breath, Your Own Risk


You enter at Y,
seeking an abandoned wheel
in a scattered archive.
Pilots, with their female destinations,
navigate messages scratched
into secretive fables.
Above the city, owls
with sweeping wings signal a warning.
The woman you seek
has a song like Siren.
She struggles against time
and inattention and rock.
Lightly her arms,
transparent and luring,
flutter like a rare lepidoptera.
But in this case,
Sirens travel in twos.
When you see one,
you must be quick
about finding the other.
The biological gears
that cause you to turn,
act like lock and key.
Howling captures angst
or angst captures howling,
either way the two
are tightly tangled.
With the woman you seek,
you know there is another
somewhere close, and
despite precautions,
the impending ambush
points you to passages ever outward.
You are nowhere.
You are faint, a stain on the darkness.
Only your breath, your own risk
is visible in the world.

Wrong Century


It is the wrong century, and old men walk,
wrapped in medicated bandages.
Those with faces aid those without.
They travel in queues, like caterpillars
in mobile cocoons. No one has wings.
No one ever develops the remarkable skill to fly,
despite their longing and hallucinations.
Off the sidewalk, to the left of the older brownstones,
a length of bandages insinuating human form
lies shriveling in the heat.
This so-called cocoon produces a shrunken mass,
indistinguishable from any other wronged skeleton.
Broken bones and particles of skull
betray the former inhabitant---
a soldier, once moving quickly in combat.
Soldiers themselves are pieces of armor.
They can be broken down into components.
When they return home, with their armor
beneath the skin, the softer parts suffocated,
they can blend in only with buildings,
metal frames, highway underpasses.
Somewhere in another country lies the soul
of this one or that; from him to "it"
and back to him before the "it"ness
squirms in again.

Corridor


glasses
grey mustache
green tie
and whatever else beneath these
seemed irrelevant.

propelling his body
down the narrow corridor,
swinging his arms
as if jumping
from one invisible handrail to another

2 unequal eyes,
acknowledging 3 or 4 more in passing,
and, on the left,
a mouth
occupying time with muscle.

watching sidewalk
disappear underfoot,
removes a watch
from his wrist,
leaves it on top
of a parking meter,
and disappears
down an alley
made of pure
regret.

First Things


Everything in child-form
demands immensity.
All playgrounds begin
with fingers and toes.
Our hearts' first spoken
things were given without regret.
The first sense of ownership
existed only to appease our hunger.
Shape and light were philosophy.
Religion was not a thing.
Faith and warmth were.
Questions and revelation
were immediate.
No notion of selfhood
was externalized.
Despite our propensity
for complicating Life
with our own broken psyches,
every Being, contained within
a once helpless form,
was made to open to immensity
and close to the suggestion
of nothingness.

Foreign Film

One figure descends
a distant fire escape
juggling awkward weight.
Pushes a closed fist
into the street.
Three buttons emerge from
instantly loosened fingers
and, as coinage, are offered
to an adjacent streetlamp.
The buttons roll past the base
and, looking briefly backward,
the figure, the breathing stain,
runs away quickly as though a lover,
liberated from abuse.
A child or small woman,
rushes from behind a closed kiosk,
steals three buttons as they lay
glittering in the lamplight,
and disappears into a sudden manhole.
Coughing announces
a nearby corridor.
       A man
     a shadow
        a lightning rod
rises from the dimly lit space.
Ice grows as
dandelions melt.

Hard Harvest

The twins have fallen together.
One tumbles and the other twirls.
One pulls to the other's push.
See them through the window glass,
there---lying flat on their backs,
all the fruit spilled from their buckets.
She waits for them to stop rolling,
to hear her muffled cry.
New apples
shiny and firm
roll outward and away
with such hopeless momentum
(boxed in,
 pulled down).
On the floors beneath and above her
only the shadow shakes
with indecisive determination.
Buried in apples rotting
so slowly, so wickedly slow,
while the rest of her,
red
bruised
and half-eaten
can no longer feel its core.

Empty Basket


I know what an empty basket looks like,
how depth is carved
        out of that nothingness---
how nothingness
is described
by an abundance of it,
            but depth is all there is ---
            depth and longing
            and the ever-echoing
            sound of need.

A house juggles
notions of home
like photographs
hide fragments of lifetime.

Housewife in Three Parts


I.  Housewife cleaning with vacuum and mirror

        Trust not thine own vision
        but reflection
        or photo
        or reflection
        reveals always
        what needs undoing.


II. Housewife moving to measure motion

        All motion happens
            before it is recorded.
        "Here" happened long ago,
            and you are actually "there" when
                    you seem to be "here".
        You have been there for some time,
          counting off floor space with lima beans.

III. Housewife polishing rock and staircase

        Elbow grease equals millennia of erosion.
        It's not the weight of the step,
                        but the regular traffic.
        If minutes bring hours and hours move months,
        her steady response to his incessant inquiries
        can absolutely dictate the rules of spacetime.
        Light bends when the corners of her mouth
        move toward a smile.
        Rock or staircase, there's always something
        devoted to elevation or descent.

Smallness


Smallest fingers,
curling toes,
new as you are to the world.
The soles of your feet, unknown to Earth.
Your head is and always will be
the heaviest part of your body,
only now you know it.
Soon you'll forget,
and only the thoughts
will seem heavy,
and occasionally, the heart.
In the interim,
seasons within seasons,
warmth, cold, or rain,
it is my body that conducts the movements,
my hands and gravity-married feet.
One day I'll be small again, and helpless,
needing someone else to do the moving.
Small boy, I wonder if you'll carry me.
Just then you smile,
and all "smallness" is gone away.

Immigration


I know you feel safe when I hold you,
but you've never known danger
or that harm can absolutely dissolve
the arms that enfold you.
It's hard being the watchman...
    so many days and nights,
burning on nothing but love and will.
Tomorrow, the same.
Next day, the same.
My arms will be your universe,
and like every living thing,
you'll want to wriggle and explore
the boundaries, and the space
you inhabit will be so small,
and Freedom, you should know,
despite your experience,
never is a small thing.
In the morning, I will rise,
and fight for you again
until we reach stronger arms,
able to enfold us in something
whose boundaries measure
more than my arms' length.

Hungry Edges


She wasn't a child.
She wasn't a girl
or a woman.

She was a centuries' old
pattern, a set of variables
subject to conditions only
she could know,
conditions under which
new things grow and burn
and grow again.

The inner pathways
that are created by endless searching,
the ones with divots in odd places
made by sudden pivoting,
have led her to discover
what must be infinity.

There are seven hours
that are possibly carefree,
then seventeen more of nothing
but hungry edges.

Inexhaustible


Inexhaustible warmth
from the confusion of numbers,
inexhaustible doubt
bred by the warming oven,
a central and curiously
unnerving energy burns.
The flowers closing
to the oncoming day,
holding tightly and turning within.
The morning glories
turn away from burning.
The women with their umbrellas
shrink as they sit by the curb,
waiting for closed transportation.
Brighter blooms have no fear.
Intensity beckons--longs for belonging.
The rain, with its lyrical motion,
ties everything together.

More Weight Than World


My path to you
through worn trains
fastened to derelict tracks
twists in such a way
that journey as entity
wields more weight
than world.

Nothing And Carry One


Calculation is endless.
Variables multiply
in existential ecstasy.
Some are added.
Others are taken away,
and division always marks creation.
He crosses the street
in a broken-down motion.
His torn coat creates
a rift in his environment,
his energy divided and subdivided.
His thoughts are scattered,
creating their own diversions
until a car horn warns him of danger.
He looks at the cursing driver
and is, for the first time, centered.
The line is drawn,
giving way to this sudden conclusion:
the symbols standing for unknowns
can disappear and reappear simultaneously.

Sexless Voyeur


burstable
percussive
organ

wooing
blood
with sultry
rhyme

exotic
expansive
rhythm

joyless
sexless
palpable
voyeur

immediate
pure,
pounding
itself
slowly
into inexistence.

Phantom Conductor


Appearing
in the distance,
his own vision
composed, first,
of nothing but steam.
A train,
powering through
the wilderness of time,
slowly gains mass
with proximity.
A phantom conductor
eager to penetrate the dark
with narrow beam,
steps down and checks
the cars for vagrant shadows
before disappearing
into the beam itself.
Massive, overwhelming,
the steam lets its last breath
as the train
sinks into the tracks,
the whistle sounding
briefly and fading.
Into the morning
he walks along the tracks,
hoping to see that conductor once more,
to lean into the beam of light
as it shines through the ethereal nature
of true night.

Stars Are Not Folded Empty Telegrams

Stars are not folded
empty telegrams.
They do not burn
in hydrostatic equilibrium
so that we may crush
and throw them away.
When the core stops burning
and what occurs is collapse,
it is clear they never existed
to grant a wish
or bring luck in falling.
What is given in message,
from opening to closing,
is that Everything is
until it isn't.

The Bullet Who is a Seashell


The chamber,
in which sound seems
to forever go 'round,
   is itself cold...
but the slow moving
  quick seeming
round, so round,
yet microscopically
odd-angled house
explodes as the wall
of a more infinite being
   is penetrated.

The bullet,
who is a seashell
hidden from the August sun,
   opens like
the fingers of a hand
delivering a final message
in magnificent color.

The Flower and the Woman


Centuries-old
in their likeness,
the flower and the woman,
both rooted in earth,
expanding underground,
reaching upward,
always in two places at once,
sometimes confusing place
with purpose.
The woman steps
down from the bus.
Maybe she has forgotten
this imagery.
Maybe her skirt is no longer
confining enough
to inspire a certain slowness.
Whatever it is,
she still opens at dawn
and closes at dusk.
She still carries each role
as petals against the elements,
still moves solemnly
from budding to older bloom
in slow mysterious time.

Staircase

The staircase
that moves through
the rooms of the quiet house
is the only structure
connecting presence
with absence.
In a kind of four-dimensional
handstand, the stairs,
in their sturdy frame,
open and close upon histories.
She hears the steps creak
with each footfall.
They cling and move as muscle.
When her back is arched,
the landings bend to meet her.
With her hand upon the railing,
she feels steadied by an ensuring arm.
When she groans with what seems
the final exhalation,
the next flight begs her furtherance.
Upon reaching the last step,
she immediately begins at the first one.
It is difficult to think
of the house without its
heart; without that deep
internal mode of transportation,
as though it, not the house, was first.

Willful Extension


She didn't have it
and couldn't reach it.
The coordinates were wrong
and the map far too worn
to render a good reading.
All she could hope was that she,
in smallness and true pulse,
was shaped into an image
of that complicated territory
and that by willful extension,
the winding features,
by feet and inches,
would lay open to legend.

Until then she would play
all the parts---
the fields,
the woods,
the road, the bridge,
the dangerous curve that nearly took her life.

She would play the parts
in manifold disguises,
rounding out sharp corners,
wearing rough grooves into smoothness.
The day that was the day of finding
would find itself surrounded by discarded
material, symbols and signals shed
to reveal only the palm of her open hand.

Witness the Disintegration of Self


I dreamed I had ended
and you had yet to begin.
I went down from rising,
other movement indicative
only of restless hibernation.

A different kind of telescopic lens
would allow you to see all things
as though they were first made,
as though You were first made,
          a flying soul---
your resting place,
more cathedral than hotel.

It is not age that brings wisdom,
  it's the falling apart
                  and beginning again.

Your Gift In This Morning Of My Heartbeat


A wonder how your fingers
have become such domesticated
beings since your mother kissed
them, tiny and new.
Now they look older than your
father's as he laid, hands
folded on his chest, in the last
space of open light.
They have been burned,
sliced, and smashed---
ironic that our fingerprints
bless everything they touch.
Everywhere, we stain creation
with our creations.
Your gift to me
in this morning of my heartbeat
is your pulling me
into your gaze so that you can
say with deliberate depth
the things that bond us
beyond belief.

Bright And Quick


Full of flame,
his fall to the floor
seemed to happen in slow motion.

The browser had closed
and coffee bled outward
in an increasing expanse
around the cup.

Birds that had gathered
on the windowsill
in the early morning light
stood oblivious to the spark
still traveling chaotically within.

Writhing in experiential burning,
he flashed bright and quick
before the body of blessing was formed,
moving through the ceilings of building and sky
as ghost from gravity.